# *After Hours*

### Selected Poems

### *by*
# Mark Bolanowski

**Blue Mustang Press**
**Boston, Massachusetts**

© 2010 by Mark Bolanowski.
All rights reserved. No part of this book may be reproduced in any form without written permission from the publishers, except by a reviewer who may quote brief passages in a review to be printed in a newspaper or magazine.

First printing

Cover image courtesy of Kevin Carden. A collection of Kevin's photography can be viewed on line at www.cardensdesign.com

Feeding Frenzy, Arms Length, and Castles in the Sand have appeared previously in the on-line poetry journal Words-Myth.

"Wasted Away" on page 23 appears courtesy of Dan Dickheiser
"Point of No Return" on page 43 appears courtesy of Payam Rajabi (payamrajabi.com)
Image on page 48 appears courtesy of VaiMoi (flickr.com)
Image on page 51 appears courtesy of Paola Mosqueda (flickr.com)

The poem "U-Haul in the Driveway" was authored by Stephanie Feldstein and appears courtesy of - and in honor of - her.

ISBN 978-1-935199-02-1
PUBLISHED BY BLUE MUSTANG PRESS
www.BlueMustangPress.com
Boston, Massachusetts

Printed in the United States of America

# *After Hours*

Selected Poems

*To
Josie and Katy —
the most precious
things in my treasure chest.*

*To them I owe
more than I will ever be
able to give.*

*And to Jamie,
the best four-legged friend I will ever have.*

## *Contents*

After Hours
All-nighter
Arm's Length
Best Ever
Better Than A Pot Of Gold
Black Hole
Born Again
Candlepower
Can't Get Enough
Castles In The Sand
Collateral Damage
Daybreak
Disingenuousness
Drones R Us
Droplet
Engraved Invitation
Eyes Resting Lightly
Feeding Frenzy
Five Hundred Seventy-two Miles
Into Thin Air
Intrepid
Life Lines
Limbo
Mixed Message
Morning Routine
No Longer Wood
No One's Home
No Wallflower
Opera At 4 AM

Petals On Paper
Physics Lesson
Point Pelee
Pristine Harmonies
Redemption
Revival
Road Game
Script
Ship Of Fools
Signed In Blood
Silence
Tangled Web
Time Machine
U-Haul in the Driveway
Undiscovered
Upper Management?
Wake
Walk
Wintry Soliloquy
Princess Shooting Star (for Josie)
String of Pearls (for Katy)
Bipps

# *After Hours*

### Selected Poems

*After Hours*

Monitor turns blue
before going dark
like sky nestling against twilight –
if only sleep came that easily
to me.

SUV's room for five
one-fifth full.
One way
conversation with talk show radio
dead ends
with press of a button.

Finger flicks switch
fake daylight
splatters on apartment-white
walls – bare.
Scattered on universal beige
carpet, stark shadows –
eight legs, four arms. Two chairs
in my place. One
always empty.

Dinner finished.
Book in one hand
glass of wine unfinished
in the other, no interest
in either.

*MARK BOLANOWSKI*

Lights out.
Match sputters,
gentle glow
flows from wick.

Shadows
more subtle. Emptiness
seeps deep within. Slowly
shrinking pool,
liquid fuel, reflects
drop of light
barely hanging on
by thread sopping last drop
of life. For an instant
I burn at both ends –
lovely light
blends with darkness.

*All-nighter*

Headlights bore
tunnel through darkness.
Me racing at one end, you still
way beyond a photon's reach.

Spun from rays, amorphous
cocoon of ersatz daytime skims
atop rivers of asphalt connecting islands
of civilization. Banks littered –
billboards tease taste buds and dreams.

My cocoon
sprays inverted silhouettes
on black satin sky –
ghostly stick people with milky coiffures
watch. Like a stone
thrown, I skip
from state to state.

Lids squeegee waves of sleep
from eyes. Wearied,
Orion reclines on West's horizon,
night's journey done.
I'm awash with envy.

*Arm's Length*

We shared a nest, once
mates, supposedly
for life.

I rippled
grey blue mirror
gliding through dawn's mist.
You watched
seeing only black and white.

I filled
moonlit air with haunting
laugh and wail,
ushered in myriad tomorrows.
You heard
not listening.

Answers elude.
Like your understanding
of me. You didn't notice
I departed
long ago.

Slow upward spiral lifts
me to where blue meets black.
The Milky Way –
perfect disguise.
You'll never think
to look here.

## MARK BOLANOWSKI

I build a new nest
alone
no farther from you than I've ever been.

*Best Ever*

Sublime alignment, perfect
circle –
that day's beginning
and end.
Identical
midnights with you
and me
taking turns
atop and beneath
each other and silk.

We untangled
grudging
need to quench
hunger and thirst
before another
mad dash to mutual ecstasy.

Your card pled –
Be Mine. Too late.
I was.
Still am. Praying
we never stop going
round and round.

*Better Than A Pot of Gold*

Storm begets rainbow.
At its end
I find your sapphire eyes
inviting – cool refuge
from life's white hot mayhem.
Verdant blades
cradle you, unveiling
curves – perfection.
Flaxen strands frame smiles
suggesting – tinge of scarlet
in lips beckoning. Allure
Sirens envy. Your radiance
dwarfs arched prism
reaching skyward. I wish
all days are rainbows
beginning, ending
with you.

*Black Hole*

I stop
signaling my presence. No sound
except echoes – my last
syllable. Epilogue
implied to those no longer
listening.

I drift
in a vacuum –
space absent neighbors.
All too familiar.
Encircling emptiness
mimics what's inside.

Tidal gravity stretches
me – now two-dimensional.
Life's contours rendered
plane.

A black hole traps, crushes
hope. My last iota
joins torrent.
Collapses
amid detritus of stars
dead along with all the wishes I made on them.

*Born Again*

until today
i shackled words
with innuendos. suffocated
friendship, love. imprisoned
me in hidden meaning.

seeking life
I gave words
face value.
stripped every one
of nuance. unfettered them
with trust.

freed,
I breathed
like it was
the first time.

AFTER HOURS

*Candlepower*

Dancing, delicate
golden glow quells darkness
and in success consumes
itself.
Is it aware?

*Can't Get Enough*

Lips touch
like nudges of butterfly wings
on a breeze.
Nerves tingling, muscles
quivering. Fervent expectation
left wanting. The taste of you
lingers, demanding to meet its source
again. Insatiable
hunger.

*AFTER HOURS*

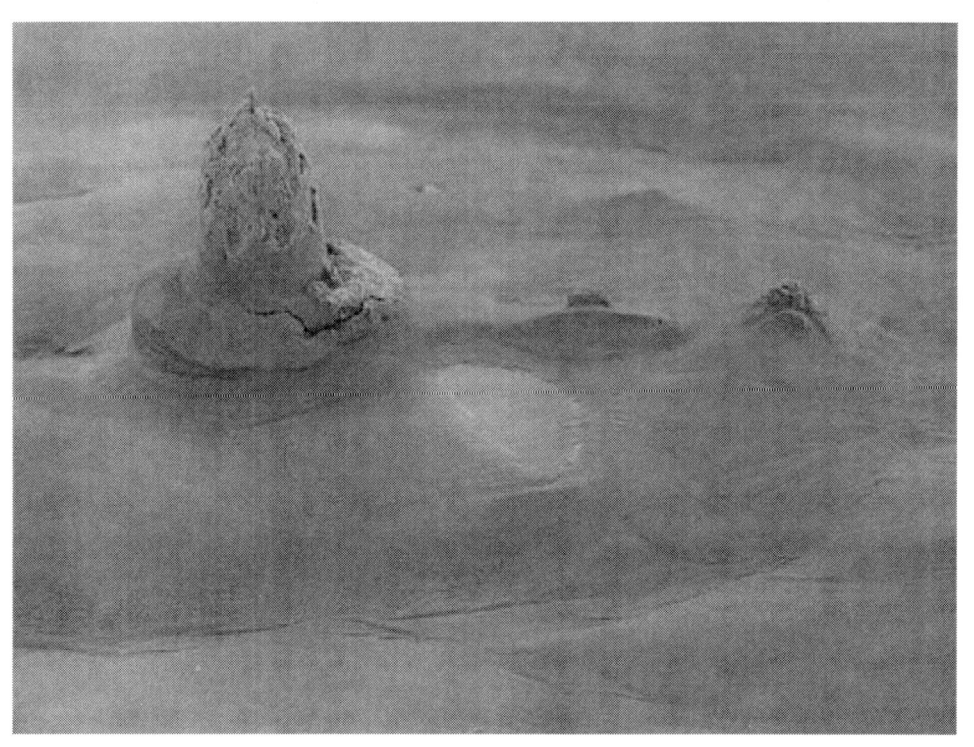

*Castles In The Sand*

Sand used to mean
castles
sculpted with hand and bucket
on the border
separating permanence and destruction. Moats
dug to protect, instead
guided waves to foundation,
turrets crumbled.

In the back
of the bus, daydream's
interrupted – annoying squawks
announce replay.
Emergency broadcast blares.
Levees weakening.

Need volunteers. Erect walls of sand.
Contain rivers
enraged by spring's thaw and rains.
Hundreds
answer the call. Me
too.

We approach mountains –
sand, empty bags –
and join the fight.

Instructions simple.

Fill sack –
three small shovels
full of sand – tie off
top, repeat
'til horn announces
convoy's arrival. Line up
side by side. Turn
left, grab bag, turn
right, hand it off.

Repeat. Keep bags streaming.
Overflow beds with hope.

Hours pass.
Idle conversation wanes
revealing the scrape
sand against metal.

Muscles scream –
silent pleas tempt
surrender. Horn blares.
Minds numb. No time to take five.
Man's stacks of sand
must rise
faster than Mother Nature's river.

We line up
human worker ants
side by side. Turn
left, grab bag, turn
right, hand it off.
Over and over. Bags stream,
beds overflow with hope.

Day flows
into evening, then midnight.
Horn blares once more.
Only words arrive.

Levees failed.

Towns
gone.  Homes and lives –
castles
lost.  We huddle.

Sand clings
to sweat, except
where rivers of sorrow inscribe
the loss.

*Collateral Damage*

Your words,
sharper than honed steel
blades, carved scars
deep – entry
through their backs
just as you planned. To strike
quick, hard – bold faced
lies
laden with intent to kill
careers.

Attacking my friends
you provoked me –
retaliation
made perfect
by stealth inherent in the obscure
source.

Oblique
angles of time and place,
randomly spaced. You can't anticipate –
your defenses are rendered moot.

Guerilla warfare.
Booby traps
fashioned with innuendos –
explosive truths
tripped by wires woven
from your lies –

lain so you shred
your own reputation.

Don't bother looking
over your shoulder, I am
no longer there.

*AFTER HOURS*

*Daybreak*

You invade my dream
with secrets
uttered softly, from lips
moistening mine.  Pleasant pressure
you atop me.  Your hair
brushes my eyes open.

My fingers trace
temptation on subtle contours
thinly veiled, suggesting
naked truth – stirring
sudden heat.

Stripped bare
lust incinerates all shreds of self-
control.  Succumbing to prurience,
we become infernos bent on ecstasy.

A blare
wrenches my eyes open,
douses the dream –
red numerals pierce waning dark.

Another day begins
with a cold shower.

*Disingenuousness*

You told me
what you wanted
me to hear.
I believed
until I found you
sans honesty –
words worth trusting in short supply.

You got
nothing but whole truth
from me.
I assumed
same in return.

I know better
now. You will get
almost as good
as you gave. I won't
yield to temptation,
become another you –
hypocrite, pathological
fountain of counterfeit truth.

To you I offer
fewest
words, nothing but truth –
meager veil of sincerity.

*Drones R Us*

Flatbeds tote
grey rectangles – pieces
of walls to be. Another floor
of airy offices – comfortable
homes to colleagues, inspiration
of productive camaraderie –
to be cubicled. One more
honeycomb
devoid of character, personality.

Too soon
workers will swarm,
filling, one by one
drab environment their minds
will mirror,
busied with routine
tasks
performed by rote.

Hive to be
exceeds speed limit
eager to siphon life from creative spirits.

MARK BOLANOWSKI

*Droplet*

Growing unhurried,
on precarious perch,
you glisten.
For an instant brighter
than any gem.
You succumb to gravity
release your grip,
embark on brief flight
to landfall. Seemingly lost
in the multitude – pond
becoming stream becoming river becoming ocean
Ripples herald your essence
as they journey to infinity.

*AFTER HOURS*

*Engraved Invitation*

Your voice penetrates
anesthesia's fog, coaxing
my mind to notice two
blue pools shimmering - sappphires amid sun drenched strands
chase remnants of induced dreams.

Scars,
some skin deep,
superficial injuries now mere
memory. Beneath these, invisible
scars she carved on my core
by violating her every word.
Gnawing residue of wounds
I've let no one see
or touch
until today.

You asked "Why
me?" In front of no one else
can I shed pretense –
plethora of affected smiles. Veils
often stretched, like me, to near transparency.
Wanting
to live, I expose the wounds
to let you see
and touch
and heal
more than skin deep.

*Eyes Resting Lightly*

Before
I transformed thoughts
to words, you understood.
Before
queries passed your lips
answers passed mine.
No need
to speak.  Your eyes rested lightly on mine.

My heart
tendered, met yours
halfway.  Our spirits mingled –
marrow touching
marrow.  Lives
entwined.  Two
became one.

In unison
we recoiled.  Promises
You made null – voided.
All it took was the twelve letters you had
to say.  I had
an affair.  Cancelled out
harmony.  Discontent
bred discord.  Cacophony
droned in the place
our song once played.

## MARK BOLANOWSKI

You vanished. I sought
anonymity amid white noise of life.
My eyes spilled
sorrow
awash with vague images –
enchantment annulled.

I imploded.
Shards collapsed, wreckage scattered.

Time tends my shattered core –
its salve guides pieces toward home.

When life wilts my will
eyelids fall, darkness
unveils the memory –
your eyes resting lightly on mine.

*Feeding Frenzy*

I struggle
to escape the cutting edge of discord
between who I am
and who the world wants me to be.
Shelter evades. I grab a blade,
peel slivers of my skin,
shape them into hors d'oeuvres, fake
smiles stuffed with flattery.
I carve my flesh,
shave the slices until they slip
into the crevices of narrow minds.
Viscera seasoned with superficial
sincerity for egos that crave fawning.
My core
covered with false confections – just dessert
for those who ignore the truth.
Me. Devoured
right before your eyes.

*Five Hundred Seventy-Two Miles*

Under covers,
years and lives shared
warms narrowing space
between us. We rest
motionless.
Then comes cruel momentum.
Condemned,
I oscillate
between earning your love
and a living.

You recede in rearview mirror.
Speedometer fixed.
Eyes dilate in front
of gray matter weighed down
by impending solitude –
a bob Foucault would admire.

Asphalt and trees
blend into race of black and green through which I reach
motionless moment
opposite
you.

Beneath a comforter
that doesn't
I shudder, chilled –
degrees of separation
intensify the ticks of time 'til I return to you.

*Into Thin Air*

Starlight mimics
your eyes. Meeting mine
only shadows
dancing among moonbeams.

Melodies land
gently. In my ears,
eager for your next note,
echoes ricochet.

Fingers brush my palm.
Your hand fits. In mine
exists nothing.

Passion glistens
in beads.
Your skin tingles. My tongue
salted by my own tears.

The path home
lined with honeysuckle – your favorite. And mine
are the only footprints.

Dreams hover
briefly. Evening's mist becomes morning's dew
and evaporates.

*AFTER HOURS*

*Intrepid*

I'm not
special, brave
she said. To me
she is quite the opposite.

I know
few who would invest
two years, spent
hours at a time, once or twice
a month, coaxing coral
sea into view.

Mural
in color submerged
beneath epidermis
wrist to shoulder.

Lower and upper
arm muscles contract
relax, like turning
of tides.

Sea
stars, horses, and dragons
spring to life.

Poised
atop her Kawasaki
green two-wheeled machine

*MARK BOLANOWSKI*

she and her one armed salt water aquarium
cruise to strip of sand
where toes can play
tag with the edge of the ocean.

*AFTER HOURS*

*MARK BOLANOWSKI*

*AFTER HOURS*

*Life Lines*

I sat, paid,
she read. Two strings of footprints –
you and me, unconnected. At first
both unaware
of the other. Invisible
forces guided our lines and arcs. Randomly
we intersected. Nonrandom
glances became passion became family.

Anniversaries
came, went, became
unnoticed, uncelebrated –
just another day
on calendar hung by pin
on wall, otherwise blank. Space
and time
interceded. You took tangent
differentiated
you from me, stretched
vow made with gold
disc placed on left ring finger
to one point away
from no return –
from vanishing.

You confess. I cry
as you apologize. We choose
to intersect. Deriving pleasure
from increasing proximity –

we become mutual asymptotes.
This time constant,
attraction narrows intervals.
Integrating, again
we become indivisible.

I used to pray
the palmist had been right.

*Limbo*

Whistles fill
moonlit air.  Faint
comes quiet chatter of steel.

Wheels
clattering on barred ribbons
stretched past invisible horizon.

Whispers of adventure.  I can't ignore
shadows assuming silhouettes –
places far away.  Dreams
coaxed to life.  Temptation pervades.

Whistles return, faded
farther away.  I hover
between surety and lure.

Whispers echo past choices –
status quo prevailing.  Again,
desire collides with fear.

Whistles die
like my nerve.

*MARK BOLANOWSKI*

*AFTER HOURS*

*Mixed Message*

Air fills with white specks.
Icy lace lands in my palm.
Hello is Good-Bye.

MARK BOLANOWSKI

*Morning Routine*

A breeze dances with wind chimes,
the evening fills with melodies –
air alive with your laughter.

Moonbeams weave
hints of you in every moment –
my soul rapt in tapestries of you.

Starlight's feint
its twinkle pale imposter of your eyes –
a field of daisies in a midnight sky.

Sunshine struggles
to warm. Thoughts of your smile heat –
all of me ablaze.

Today begins like too many yesterdays.

At the well
        eyes closed,
                hand open,
                        coin falling,

wishing

you hear my spirit sing
when you smile, your eyes seek mine
as days begin and end, you find love
in my arms.

*AFTER HOURS*

MARK BOLANOWSKI

*No Longer Wood*

Air and earth once cool
beneath deep green canopy.
Hot macadam burns.

*AFTER HOURS*

*No One's Home*

I need proof,
much more proof.
One hundred isn't enough
to smother
consciousness with frail veils of sleep.

Propped atop finger tips, empty bottle
mirrors sack of skin
I am, holding warmth and shape, but not
for long. I fell
into traps I set
for me.

You were young.
We played, laughed,
not often enough. I thought
there'd be other days.

I chased salary, promotions,
feigned importance.
Fed ego, starved you,
love felt not shared. Full time,
I droned –
dawn to dark rushes in ever deepening rut.
I let you slip away.

Providing in absentia –
perfect penance.
Irony kindles smiles

quickly doused.
Regret trickles,
eyes to cheeks to lips.

Tears tinged with love
evanesce.  Freed, affection rides
a breeze, caresses your cheek –
kisses from Dad.  Finally
where they belong.

The *we* that could have been taunts
while swimming in ethanol.
My sigh,
exposed by predawn chill
mocks me –
there, then not.

Bone dry.

*AFTER HOURS*

*No Wallflower*

Twirling pairs trace rhythms
across the floor. She sits,
half filling a loveseat
someone placed away from gaiety.

Her stare wanders
past panes reflecting
revelry. Behind impassive eyes
memories of him stretch past horizon –
pearls on the thread of her life.
Her mind caresses
each opalescence, traveling back
to that first dance. Awkward
until they met –
kindred rhythms crossing lines
between girl and boy,
adolescent and adult,
autonomy and union.
She watches
memory and reflection
an audience of one
in neither.

Warm breath
imbues reminiscing with her name, enticing
her back to the present. He enfolds her.
Together they trace lives
entwined.

*AFTER HOURS*

*Opera At 4 AM*

Pre-alarm
cries drag me,
unwilling, into today.

Eyes squeezed
shut, covers pulled
around my neck
to repel morning
chill.

First two
then three
and now at least four sopranos –
sirens pronounce the emergency.

Right to left
I roll to point ears
opposite cacophony that pierces dark.

Blares of police
cruisers joined by three tenors –
ambulances race to mangled bodies
on razor thin edge
separating life from death.

It's two hours
before alarm is set
to sound off. Three
hours until I punch in.

Odd two-part harmonies enhanced
by baritones and base –
two fire engines and Medevac chopper
complete the chords.

Covers tossed
aside. Bared
feet chilled by floor.
No need for snooze button
this morning. Even back way will be slow go.

*Petals on Paper*

My pen left
silent impressions –
black and blue
indentations. Moments
absent inspiration.

Years' worth
of debris – tortured
metaphors scratched
on thin sheets. Now crumpled
ideas – abandoned
dreams spill over the rim.

My eyes rummage
the rectangle, blank, staring
back – reflecting
white noise of life
ricocheting between ears. Thoughts
thwarted.

Fingers trace
paper's edge. Cut,
I bleed. Red
invades white. Exposed,
nerves fire. Pain
quiets noise.

*MARK BOLANOWSKI*

Fingers imbue letters
pooling into words –
delicate images on paper,
like petals. Abundant
color, fragrance.
Alive.

*Physics Lesson*

two bodies
    bundled
        strings of energy
            traversing space,
                life on vectors converging
                    at a ninety degrees
                        to a point
                            they'll both occupy
                                perhaps for the instant
                                of contact
                            and recoil perhaps
                      for an instant
                  before mutual annihilation
              perhaps more than an instant
            because
            mutual attraction
        holds them
    together

MARK BOLANOWSKI

*Point Pelee*

moonlit sand
its gentle glisten
broken. strings of impressions
edges and details softened
by wind, wave –
frangible residue of solitary souls.

rare doublets
parallel strings invade
domain, taunting
with image of what could be
and what was.

memories of latter
rekindle chill, despair
that seeps deep
displaces hope
tempts surrender.

years ago
i found stick
on same strip of sand
i trod
now. then
this slender length of wood
polished by wind whipped sand
and water
caught toes, sent face

*AFTER HOURS*

first into sand
then wake. wet
i grabbed wooden offender
cocked arm
to fling it out to sea.

its smooth surface
captured by hand and eyes
tactile and visual
survey of gentle curves
sapped
anger. diffused
i kept stick
its simple beauty –
subtle
touch of magic –
able to calm and inspire
until tonight.

i gave
you took
all but last shirt.
with nothing else left
on my back, i ceased
being easy
source of green
paper you held
more important than i.
you stretched
gold encircled bond
past breaking point with silence.
the shoulder
once refuge –
now sucking mercury
below absolute zero.

## MARK BOLANOWSKI

stick in hand
once more
it and i
make the only impressions
in sand tonight. i leave
stick where it entered
my life.
where it might enter
someone else's.

one last peek
over shoulder, my impressions
lead toward wake
where they
and i go out with the tide.

*AFTER HOURS*

*Pristine Harmonies*

Sun
hovers
half beneath almost hidden
horizon. I can't discern
Crayola sky from hills
emblazoned by Fall –
maples and clouds alike.

Sunset
paints evening
indigo, unveiling
glistening ballet,
planets and galaxies
pirouette, enticing tomorrow.

Stars escort today to yesterday.

Midnight
reprise portrayed for two
miles and mountains
apart. Spirits
threaded through wishing
star's soft light. Nocturnal talisman
illuminates memory. Behind eyelids
you smile, your arms invite.
Entangled, we merge.

*Redemption*

Imprisoned in blistering labyrinth
lies molten form of mother earth
On occasion she stretches
cracks crust, sheds shackles.
Surfacing, she drapes all
in roiling red, leaves death
in her smoldering wake.

Plumes – spent fury –
convert sky blue
to gray. Her unobstructed view
moot; all she sees
is desolate obsidian left behind.

Regret
floods her eyes
falls
wets wound,
begins healing.

Showering self
with mother's love, covering
self in blanket of light,
she conceives
new life in her ashes.

*Revival*

Weathered
memories rendered frail
faint,
by time,
life, lie dormant, silent.
until smile, hello
arrive from an old friend
peel away pallor,
restore brilliance.
What was
faded, cold
now
bright, warm.
And,
If only for a while,
What was,
Is.

*MARK BOLANOWSKI*

*AFTER HOURS*

*Road Game*

Work week ends, turning
left from lot
not right –
away from home. I fall
in line of one
of dozens of caravans –
high schools on the move.

Team colors sprout from rows –
squared windows
framed in yellow. Pom poms
stretched taut by slipstream –
ribbon bouquets glide
atop asphalt.

Parents, siblings, neighbors fill
cars, SUVs, vans strung
like kite tail for wheeled boxes
filled with uniformed teens –
players, musicians, cheerleaders, all
too eager to strut their stuff.

Sun first touches horizon
as referee signals kickoff.
Not quite hot
dog and chocolate downed
before whistles blow second play
dead.

I find my seat –
unnumbered segment of aluminum
between the fifty
and those setting the beat
with sticks on skin –
amid blue and gold
sea of which I am part.

Body temp drops,
its heat source no match
for near winter chill
riding north wind.

Halftime
lines for concessions and Johnies
On The Spot more like
grains of sand sliding
to narrow port between top
and bottom of hourglass.

Final whistle
liberates pent up delight
on our bench
and side of the field.

Blue and gold caravan retraces
steps. Horns
honked all the way
home –
sounds of victory
riding north wind.

*Script*

White coat and stethoscope adorn
form giving voice
to verdict – life
rendered moot.

I have one more
act – less than
year of lines for players
to read. All roles
open. Cattle call
placed in Want Ads
weeks ago.

I stare
at no shows, stage
filled with no one waiting
in the wings. I exit stage
left – confined in solitude.
Tamper proof
cap lies, like me, upside down
next to bottle, upright,
empty, like glass
in my hand. White
pills at work.

Eyelids fall –
silence
cues. Curtain
closes.

*Ship Of Fools*

No sense
trying to right
ship torpedoed
from within. Weapons
targeted, armed, fired –
aimed to eliminate
jeopardy to grand plan
authored by self empowered
few who seek space
unfettered by fact,
logic, honesty. Those
possessing these three
hit point blank.

Clueless few
failed to notice proximity
of target and hull –
latter forged by former.
Ruthless few
celebrate "success," unaware
water displaces
air into which they proclaim
victory.

Water level rises
faster than the few can
make repairs. Struggling
to not inhale
water

the few beseech those
they eliminated. Pleas fall
on dead ears.

No avoiding
next stop –
Davey Jones' Locker.
Culprit and innocent
victim, alike
only in fate.

*AFTER HOURS*

*Signed In Blood*

Superficial, perfect
rendering of its source –
my reflection
on solid silver
rectangle. Engraved.
my initials dangled
from ring – high school graduation
gift, I soon spoiled with status
symbols absent substance –
like me. Once prideful,
collecting short, toothed bars,
metallic openers
of houses, cars, offices. Spaces
accumulated in vain
attempt to fill
life and me devoid –
no love given or taken.

Spaces now rusting, rotting,
empty save one. As is the ring.
Its last denizen ignites engine
reluctant to grant my request to outrace
the past suffocating
with shame I earned.
Shame I must shed.

I was indifferent – deliberately
ignoring all
except those who could help

me. Shallow.
Selfish core barely covered
with skin deep compassion
offered only long enough
to get what I wanted. I used everyone
around me. Family and friends, all
left me where I belong.

Alone. Choking
on the shame. I can't swallow
no matter how stiff the drink.

Speedometer and breath
twice the legal limit. Squealing
tires strain to parallel white stripes.
Road turns. I don't.

Metal and flesh meet cement.
Beyond repair, I watch
my initials dangle,
reflecting shallow red stream –
me, emptied
on asphalt, signing away
my life on the dotted white line.

*AFTER HOURS*

*Silence*

parking lot conversation
ended. parting
you pointed
at my phone –
"later" you said.

evening nudges afternoon
light fades
petals quiver
in the breeze – dusk's ballet
of color. shimmering
earthbound rainbow.

phone's beep
startles heart
tingles skin –
false alarm.
charge complete.

my hands tremble
attempt to feel
the blossoms, like your skin
brushing against mine.

like your breath
caressing my ear, enticing
songs, filling midnight
air with unexpected warmth.

I stare,
mimicking clock's hands,
straight up.
starlight diffracted
by salted pools.

my mind, rapt
in the tapestry that is you,
floats in realms between reality
and dreams – sleep's
restless refuge.

you said
you'd call.
my phone never sang
your ring tone.

*AFTER HOURS*

MARK BOLANOWSKI

*Tangled Web*

Pearls of dawn adorn
threads I wove last night.
Dainty tapestry laced with danger.
Sunrise dispels warning
petals unfurl a welcome –
nascent day.
Prey enticed
by nectars' fragrant promise
snare themselves.
Entrée and dessert
in the bag,
I bask in my cunning.
Zephyrs brush a blossom,
shake me loose.
A purple martin catches my fall.
Light vanishes
moist walls surround, collapse.
Trapped, I wait.

*Time Machine*

Walls stretch, skyward
extensions, seamless
with cobbled alleys. I'm surrounded
by stone. Old
stone surprising my fingertips
with warmth – enduring
residue of Earth's origin.

I'm channeled
by the stone, deeper in catacombs
of time. Past
a doorway enticing
more than others. Stepping
across ancient threshold, I'm transported –
eight hundred years
ago.

I'm embraced
by timbers, settling
with and into
the Earth, bending
like elbows
raising pints, welcoming
like faces
smiling. Scene reprised
each of a quarter million
yesterdays, and today –
reminder and lure.

*MARK BOLANOWSKI*

Time's inexorable march – imperceptible
passerby here.
Spirits gathering
over centuries, lingering
in the moment long enough to choose
dissolution of my soul,
now mingling, indistinguishable
among myriad others. I am
home.

*AFTER HOURS*

*U-Haul in the Driveway*
          by Stephanie Feldstein

Labyrinthine, living
room filled with boxes
stacked in Tetris
formations, I shift
pieces –
my life, fitting
together neatly, spiraling
upward like Jack's beanstalk
into unknown lands.

Forget images –
butterflies bursting
from cocoons, or flowers
blooming under nurturing rays
in reverence to life anew.

Picture Punxsutawney Phil
hesitant, sidling
out of his burrow, nose
twitching, testing
the air – waiting
to see if he's banished
to frosty solitude
or welcomed by warmth.

*Undiscovered*

Karyoke
queen – stardom
stuck in anonymity. Instead
of flowers tossed
on her stage, keratin
strands – natural
and not
shades of blond, brown, black –
fall at her feet.
As deft fingers guide
her scissors to snip
locks to lengths just right
she sings along with Top 40
radio. Hit
on pitch, each note
a work of art
drowned
in the din of the salon.

*AFTER HOURS*

*Upper Management?*

It is
10:00 AM Friday.
Start of one
of year's fifty-two
conclaves – self appointed
leaders gathered. No IQ
within forty points of mine.

Six surround table. In front
of each, agenda
strewn with the mundane. Items
collective intellect
struggles to grasp. The obvious
escapes the meager
minds assembled. Each weak
ego absent self-
esteem, confidence. Unwilling
to accept reality. Diameter
of each approaches infinity – universe's
closest approximation of absolute vacuum.

Computer beeps arrival –
"invitation" to impromptu
program review
in thirty minutes. No time
to prepare. Nothing
new. Door closes
behind me. Cold, arid
version of the bends

precedes flaccid paralysis,
anoxia that still
my vocal chords, dull
my mind – eliminate
threat. I pose
as comfortably numb
until it is time to leave.

*Wake*

Into life
I sailed, hold full,
cargo precious –
laughter, happiness, optimism, hope.
My course plotted, bearing
maintained by instinct, dead
reckoning – generosity.

I gave
words, time, compassion, love –
me –
to all I met. My naiveté
exposed. Too
few recipients reciprocated.
Absent recompense, I lightened –
water line dropped.

My wake, once
unbroken string churning
eddies stretched to the horizon. Fleeting
ripples,
now scant, record
my passing.

Selfish
souls who took me
for granted
pass by my office –
as at a wake
looking through open lid.

Cargo gone,
ballast
now the weight of emptiness.
Alone

I drift
unremembered
on a forgotten sea.

*AFTER HOURS*

*Walk*

Cloud's shrouds loom
low, vapor saps warmth and color
graveyard grey. Petals, leaves,
lives spent,
lie dormant and dank.
Like me.

My footfalls follow narrowing way.
What was recedes,
unceasingly, becomes less
than silhouette.
I'm engulfed by dreams.

My dreams.
Of love, innate, complete,
imbuing moments with serenity
before she smashed it
to bits on life's rock-strewn shore.
Laid my heart waste
by ebbing tide. I embrace shattered shell,
discover I hold nothing. Invisible
shards scar
without drawing blood.

Trail turns. Through scant openings
sunlight coaxes
hints of color. Above tree line,
my eyes meet fields
afire, wildflowers weave

earthbound rainbows – fragrant
tapestries caress
senses. Aroused,
emotions shed self-imposed exile.

I pass
your favorite spot. Like always
you smile. This time
I notice. My face remembers how.
Blossoms turn envy green.

Path widens
up ahead, your footprints converge
with mine. Your fingers mingle
with mine. One touch –
invisible scars begin to heal.

*Wintry Soliloquy*

Swirling white.
Silent ballets
danced just for me,
icy lace adorns all
I can see. Past
reflected – moments
nearly motionless
in space and time.

Words, laughs, tears.
Touches. Each
rides its own flake. Pristine
reflections – every instant
with you, now nestled
in front of me. Frozen fresco
glistening. Dreams
displayed on fresh plaster.

*AFTER HOURS*

*Princess Shooting Star*

The whole of you fits
neatly in my lap.
 I wish upon your star.  Knowing
 molding life isn't like shaping clay,
  that we can't stay in this moment forever,
   I wish upon your star.

After
 each laughter-filled mile traveled side-by-side
  in the orbit of a tire swing,
   each enchanting story
    painted in my mind by your voice,
     each glissade and pirouette
      made graceful by you en pointe,
       each arc of a ball ending
        in our leather-covered hands,
         each bob of a loon
          riding ripples from our canoe,
           each opponent moaning in defeat
            that rockets off your racquet,
             each stream of electrons displaying
              the instant message from you,
               each moonrise swelling the past
                shrinking our precious time
                 together,
                  I wish upon your star.

        Star that lights your path to womanhood.
         And if you listen

   closely
you'll hear it whispering my wish

   that all your wishes come true.

*String Of Pearls*

Tucked
in my arms, gentle
weight – your head
on my shoulder
we embark. Nightly
journey toward an infant's dreams.
I talk, sing. You cry, sigh,
and find them.

Deftly touched,
your perfect pass
nudged by the foot of a teammate
eludes a diving goalie's outstretched fingertips.

Sharp pops.
Your volleys zip past
lunging opponents groaning,
their flailing racquets meet only air.

Light
feet skipping,
you accelerate toward the finish line.
Foes pant, desperate to keep pace.

Smile
sparkling, quips
instantly fill the room with merriment.

Source
of my cherished collection –
hugs, made perfect by your soft sigh
"saying" I love you too.

Memories of you stretch to the horizon.
Unbroken thread
of moments. I traverse
back in time, surrounded by treasure –
time spent with you.

*Bipps*

When he was
one, pet psychic said
"He misses you when you're gone."

His own tail
wagged my dog, torso
swaying to satisfy
Newton's Third Law of Motion –
his way of saying
"I'm glad you're home."

No lap dog was he
yet he sought mine
wherever my torso and thighs formed
an L.  There
he'd settle
warm, relaxed, happy –
as he made me.

We would seek
dreamland together, he in space
between my knees
warm, relaxed, happy –
as he made me.  Throughout
night
we'd match formations
doglegs right
and doglegs left.

He turned nine
when cancer turned on him,
slowly sapping bounce, vigor,
life. But not
spirit – afire.

Ever evident
in his eyes
until they closed
the last time. He in my lap
warm, relaxed, happy –
as he still tried to make me.

It's dark.
Seeking dreamland
the space between my knees
empty. I lie
cold, restless, remembering
what the psychic said.
Sorrow wets my pillow.

*AFTER HOURS*

*AFTER HOURS*

*Thanks –*

This journey began in fifth grade when a poetry assignment led to a visit with the principal and my parents. It seems my words caused some to fret about my view of the world and life. This memory remains, still in present tense, and until a few years ago dissuaded me from writing.

My pen lay dormant until an urge coaxed me to visit a chain bookstore in Ann Arbor where I wandered into a group of writers who once a week shared and critiqued each others' wares. Pat, Karen, Edd, Jeff, Lois, Robin, Ray, Bob, Noelle, Cynthia and so many others taught me to trust my instincts and two truisms: Show, don't Tell; and avoid adverbs like the plague. Their recipe blended critique and compassion in perfect proportion.

I owe a special debt to Cynthia Allar and Stephanie Feldstein – successful poets in their own right who saw something worth their time and effort. Together they were my binary North Star, showing the way whenever I was smart enough to pay attention. Their gentle glow and touch gave me courage to reach for my dream.

I am grateful for three dear friends – Marissa Tallington, Jeffrey Martin, and Gill Hartley – who encouraged me to believe that I just might have the talent that I hoped I had.

I am thankful for the richness and variety in nature and people – idiosyncrasies and all – for supplying the moments and images that inspired the words and metaphors that fill the preceding pages.

Finally, I must thank Karen and Eric French for pointing me in the direction of Blue Mustang Press, and Walter and everyone at Blue Mustang Press for taking a chance on me.

*AFTER HOURS*